Stratford Library Association
2203 Main Street
Stratford, CT 06615
203-385-4160

W9-AMM-553

GHANA

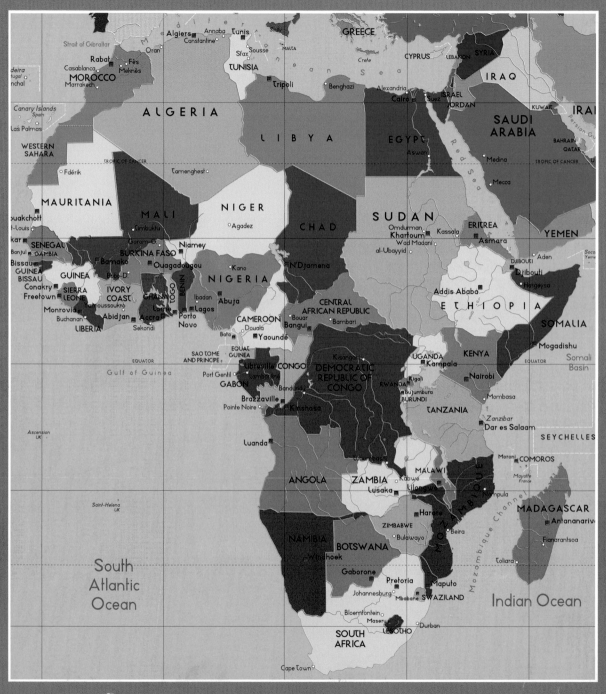

GHANA

Barbara Aoki Poisson

Mason Crest Publishers
Philadelphia

Produced by OTTN Publishing, Stockton, N.J.

Mason Crest Publishers
370 Reed Road
Broomall, PA 19008
www.masoncrest.com

Copyright © 2005 by Mason Crest Publishers. All rights reserved.
Printed and bound in the Hashemite Kingdom of Jordan.

3 5 7 9 8 6 4 2

Library of Congress Cataloging-in-Publication Data

Poisson, Barbara Aoki.
  Ghana / Barbara Aoki Poisson.
      p. cm. — (Africa)
  Includes bibliographical references and index.
  ISBN 1-59084-814-4
  1. Ghana—Juvenile literature. I. Title. II. Series.
  DT510.P65 2004
  966.7—dc22

                                                    2004007104

Africa: **Facts and Figures**	**Ghana**	**South Africa**
	Ivory Coast	**Tanzania**
Burundi	**Kenya**	**Uganda**
Democratic Republic **of the Congo**	**Nigeria**	**Zimbabwe**
Ethiopia	**Rwanda**	

Table of Contents

Africa: Continent in the Balance

Robert I. Rotberg

Africa is the cradle of humankind, but for millennia it was off the familiar, beaten path of global commerce and discovery. Its many peoples therefore developed largely apart from the diffusion of modern knowledge and the spread of technological innovation until the 17th through 19th centuries. With the coming to Africa of the book, the wheel, the hoe, and the modern rifle and cannon, foreigners also brought the vastly destructive transatlantic slave trade, oppression, discrimination, and onerous colonial rule. Emerging from that crucible of European rule, Africans created nationalistic movements and then claimed their numerous national independences in the 1960s. The result is the world's largest continental assembly of new countries.

There are 53 members of the African Union, a regional political grouping, and 48 of those nations lie south of the Sahara. Fifteen of them, including mighty Ethiopia, are landlocked, making international trade and economic growth that much more arduous and expensive. Access to navigable rivers is limited, natural harbors are few, soils are poor and thin, several countries largely consist of miles and miles of sand, and tropical diseases have sapped the strength and productivity of innumerable millions. Being landlocked, having few resources (although countries along Africa's west coast have tapped into deep offshore petroleum and gas reservoirs), and being beset by malaria, tuberculosis, schistosomiasis, AIDS, and many other maladies has kept much of Africa poor for centuries.

Thirty-two of the world's poorest 44 countries are African. Hunger is common. So is rapid deforestation and desertification. Unemployment rates are often over 50 percent, for jobs are few—even in agriculture. Where Africa once

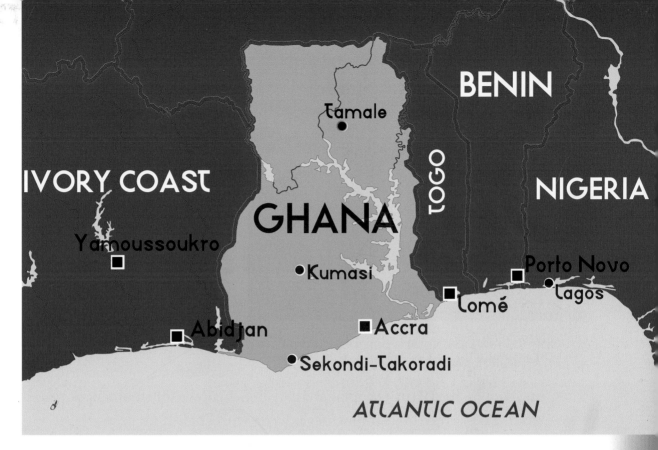

Bordering the Gulf of Guinea, the West African country of Ghana used to be called the Gold Coast for its deposits of the precious mineral.

was a land of small villages and a few large cities, with almost everyone engaged in growing grain or root crops or grazing cattle, camels, sheep, and goats, today more than half of all the more than 750 million Africans, especially those who live south of the Sahara, reside in towns and cities. Traditional agriculture hardly pays, and a number of countries in Africa—particularly the smaller and more fragile ones—can no longer feed themselves.

There is not one Africa, for the continent is full of contradictions and variety. Of the 675 million people living south of the Sahara, at least 130 million live in Nigeria, 67 million in Ethiopia, 55 million in the Democratic Republic of the

Only Ashanti chiefs are permitted to sit on an elephant stool.

Congo, and 45 million in South Africa. By contrast, tiny Djibouti and Equatorial Guinea have fewer than 1 million people each, and prosperous Botswana and Namibia each are under 2 million in population. Within some countries, even medium-sized ones like Zambia (11 million), there are a plethora of distinct ethnic groups speaking separate languages. Zambia, typical with its multitude of competing entities, has 70 such peoples, roughly broken down into four language and cultural zones. Three of those languages jostle with English for primacy.

Given the kaleidoscopic quality of African culture and deep-grained poverty, it is no wonder that Africa has developed economically and politically less rapidly than other regions. Since independence from colonial rule, weak governance has also plagued Africa and contributed significantly to the widespread poverty of its peoples. Only Botswana and offshore Mauritius have been governed democratically without interruption since independence. Both are among Africa's wealthiest countries, too, thanks to the steady application of good governance.

Aside from those two nations, and South Africa, Africa has been a continent of coups since 1960, with massive and oil-rich Nigeria suffering incessant periods of harsh, corrupt, autocratic military rule. Nearly every other country on or around the continent, small and large, has been plagued by similar bouts of instability and dictatorial rule. In the 1970s and 1980s Idi Amin ruled Uganda capriciously and Jean-Bedel Bokassa proclaimed himself emperor of the Central African Republic. Macias Nguema of Equatorial Guinea was another in that same mold. More recently Daniel arap Moi held Kenya in thrall and Robert Mugabe has imposed himself on once-prosperous Zimbabwe. In both of those cases, as in the case of Gnassingbe Eyadema in Togo and the late Mobutu Sese Seko in Congo, these presidents stole wildly and drove entire peoples and their nations into penury. Corruption is common in Africa, and so are a weak rule-of-law framework, misplaced development, high expenditures on soldiers and low expenditures on health and education, and a widespread (but not universal) refusal on the part of leaders to work well for their followers and citizens.

Conflict between groups within countries has also been common in Africa. More than 12 million Africans have been killed in the civil wars of Africa since 1990, with more than 3 million losing their lives in Congo and more than 2 million in the Sudan. War between north and south has been constant in the Sudan since 1981. In 2003 there were serious ongoing hostilities in northeastern Congo, Burundi, Angola, Liberia, Guinea, Ivory Coast, the Central African Republic, and Guinea-Bissau, and a coup (later reversed) in São Tomé and Príncipe.

Despite such dangers, despotism, and decay, Africa is improving. Botswana and Mauritius, now joined by South Africa, Senegal, Kenya, and Ghana, are beacons of democratic growth and enlightened rule. Uganda and Senegal are taking the lead in combating and reducing the spread of AIDS, and others are following. There are serious signs of the kinds of progressive economic policy changes that might lead to prosperity for more of Africa's peoples. The trajectory in Africa is positive.

From its beaches to its rain forests, Ghana's topography is diverse. (Opposite) Two Ghanaian children help load cocoa pods into a basket during harvest. (Right) A decoratively painted boat floats on the Volta River, which extends for 1,000 miles (1,609 kilometers).

1 Land of Natural Wonders

A VIBRANT LAND of dramatic beauty, Ghana boasts a great variety of natural wonders. From sandy coastal beaches in the south, to lush rain forests in the central region, to vast rolling *savanna* in the north, Ghana captures the diverse landscape of Africa in an area that is slightly smaller than the state of Oregon.

Located in West Africa, the Republic of Ghana borders the Gulf of Guinea to the south. Ghana's southernmost point, Cape Three Points, is just over four degrees of latitude north of the equator. The Prime Meridian, which passes through Greenwich, England, also passes through the southeastern part of Ghana at Tema. Ghana shares land borders with Burkina Faso to the north, Ivory Coast (Côte d'Ivoire) to the west, and Togo to the east.

Most of Ghana is low-lying and flat; about half of the country lies less than 500 feet (152 meters) above sea level. The landscape is dissected by a number of rivers and streams, most of which can be traveled only by canoe. The 1,000-mile (1,609-kilometer) Volta River, formed by the union of the Black Volta and White Volta, is Ghana's largest river system.

Geographical Regions

Ghana can be divided into five geographical regions, each with its own distinct characteristics. The coastal plain is a skinny strip of land that runs along the Gulf of Guinea. The sandy beaches of the coast give way to a lush tropical forest belt that covers about one-third of the country. To the north of the forest zone lie the savanna high plains, a dry grassy region with few trees that covers another third of the country. Located on the eastern border is a mountainous region dominated by the Akwapim-Togo ranges. The arid Volta Basin, in central Ghana, is the country's largest geographical region.

The 335-mile (539-km) coastline is comprised mainly of sandy beaches that merge into scrub-dotted plains. The Ghanaian coast has no natural harbors and the strong surf creates numerous lagoons, changing the landscape constantly. This region is flat and featureless, and the primary occupation of people who live along the coast is fishing. The Volta Delta extends into the Gulf of Guinea in the southeast corner of Ghana. Farmers grow shallots, corn, and *cassava* (tapioca) in this moist region. Coconut palms, from which *copra* is made, also grow well in the sandy delta, and Ghanaians harvest salt from the dried beds of the lagoons. Accra, Ghana's capital city, is located on the coastal plain. The hilly plains east of Accra are favored areas for agriculture, while to the west the land is mostly flat savanna.

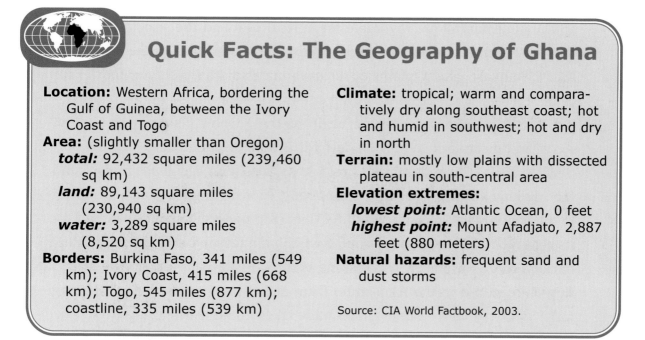

Quick Facts: The Geography of Ghana

Location: Western Africa, bordering the Gulf of Guinea, between the Ivory Coast and Togo

Area: (slightly smaller than Oregon)
  total: 92,432 square miles (239,460 sq km)
  land: 89,143 square miles (230,940 sq km)
  water: 3,289 square miles (8,520 sq km)

Borders: Burkina Faso, 341 miles (549 km); Ivory Coast, 415 miles (668 km); Togo, 545 miles (877 km); coastline, 335 miles (539 km)

Climate: tropical; warm and comparatively dry along southeast coast; hot and humid in southwest; hot and dry in north

Terrain: mostly low plains with dissected plateau in south-central area

Elevation extremes:
  lowest point: Atlantic Ocean, 0 feet
  highest point: Mount Afadjato, 2,887 feet (880 meters)

Natural hazards: frequent sand and dust storms

Source: CIA World Factbook, 2003.

The forests of Ghana are rich with timber and minerals. Tropical rain forests lie to the south and gradually give way to the savannas of the north. Occupying a large area in southwestern Ghana is the triangular-shaped Kwahu Plateau, which divides the forest belt and savanna regions. The plateau also separates the rivers in western Ghana that flow due south from the Volta River system in the east. The Ashanti uplands begin at the foot of the Kwahu Plateau in the north and extend into the lowlands in the south. This region is the country's primary producer of cocoa, minerals, and timber.

The savanna high plains region occupies the northern and northwestern part of Ghana. The terrain consists largely of a *dissected plateau* averaging between 492 and 984 feet (150 and 300 meters) in elevation. Soil conditions and annual rainfall are favorable for agriculture, and the scarcity of *tsetse flies* has resulted in a much higher population than that of the arid Volta Basin. The vast, grassy plains of the savanna also offer plenty of fodder for cattle. Livestock raising and farming are major occupations in this region.

The Akwapim-Togo ranges begin at the Kwahu Plateau just west of Accra and meander in a northeasterly direction, eventually crossing the border into Togo. This mountainous region is dense with *deciduous* forests, and the higher elevations provide a generally cooler climate. Ghana's highest point, Mount Afadjato, ascends 2,887 feet (880 meters) tall and is famed for its beautiful waterfalls. In the southeast, the ranges are cut in half by a deep, narrow gorge formed by the rushing waters of the Volta River. The river's flow is captured in the Akosombo Dam at the head of the gorge, forming Lake Volta, one of the largest man-made lakes in the world.

The Volta Basin occupies about 45 percent of Ghana's land surface. Located in the center of the country, the low-lying basin stretches from near the city of Tamale in the north to the mouth of the Volta River in the south, and serves as the country's primary drainage system. With a dry climate and generally poor soil conditions, the basin's most common vegetation is savanna. Due to the scarcity of water and the presence of tsetse flies, not many people live in the basin.

The Afram Plains, located in the southeastern corner of the Volta Basin, feature the country's lowest elevation as well as the highest levels of rainfall in the region. With an average elevation of about 344 feet (105 meters) and annual rainfall of around 50 inches (127 cm), the plains are often turned into swamps during the rainy seasons. The construction of the Akosombo Dam during the mid-1960s resulted in much of the Afram Plains being submerged beneath Lake Volta.

Climate

Ghana's climate is tropical with temperatures averaging between 78°F (26°C) and 84°F (29°C). In most areas, March has the highest temperatures and August has the lowest. Ghana has greater variations in rainfall than variations in temperature. During heavy rains, flooding is common in many areas while drought plagues the rest of the country. In general, the southeast coastline is warm and fairly dry, the southwest is hot and humid, and the northern regions are hot and dry.

The temperature and aridity of Ghana are affected by the harmattan, a hot, dry wind that blows down from the Sahara Desert. The regions north of the Kwahu Plateau have two distinct seasons—rainy and dry. From about November to late March, the harmattan season brings hot, dry days and relatively cool nights. The dry season is followed by the rainy season, which reaches its peak in late August or early September. South of the plateau, there are two rainy seasons and two dry seasons. Heavy rains occur from April to late June or early July, followed by a dry period. The second rainy season runs from September to November, then the harmattan blows in another dry spell during December or January. Rainfall in Ghana is often unpredictable, however, and doesn't always follow the expected patterns. Droughts are common during the rainy season, and flooding can occur during the dry season.

Annual rainfall in Ghana averages between about 43 inches (110 cm) in the north and about 83 inches (210 cm) in the southeast. The heaviest

Two boys go for a run along a beach near Accra. Temperatures are warm year-round in Ghana because of its location near the equator.

rains, averaging about 85 inches (215 cm) a year, occur around the city of Axim in the southwest corner of the country. Flooding is a major problem particularly along the coastline. In June 2001, a flash flood left at least two dead and about 100,000 people homeless in Accra.

Plants and Animals

Ghana is home to a diverse array of plant and animal life. As of recent counts, there are about 3,725 plant species, as well as 90 fish, 206 *breeding bird*, 222 mammal, and 164 reptile and amphibian species dwelling within the country's borders.

Ghana was once covered in forest, but due to agricultural clearing and industry, the forest zone now only covers about 30 percent of the land. There are two types of forest in the country: the humid rain forests of the south and the drier savanna forests of the north. Almost 700 different species of trees grow in the forests, including *khaya* (African mahogany), kapok (silk-cotton), and baobab, a tropical tree with a bulky trunk and spindly limbs. A variety of exotic flowers, including many rare species of orchids, also flourish in the woodlands. Trees and plants are important sources of food, fuel, medicine, and export products. However, widespread logging and, more recently, mining threaten the delicate balance of the ecosystem.

The Upper Guinea Forest, which spans from Guinea through Ghana to western Togo, is a nature lover's paradise. Its native mammals include leopards, lions, hyenas, hippopotamus, buffaloes, elephants, forest hogs, antelopes, and monkeys. The bird population is particularly diverse, with exotic species like parrots, bee-eaters, blue plantain-eaters, hornbills, hummingbirds, and raptors. Nearly as diverse is the reptile population, which includes crocodiles, cobras, pythons, vipers, and adders.

Ghana's forests are part of the Guinean Forests of West Africa *biodiversity hotspot*, which provides vital refuge for 70 threatened species. These include the forest elephant, bongo (large forest antelope), giant forest hog, over 20 endangered butterflies, and 3 of the world's 25 most-endangered monkey species.

Conservationists are striving to protect and preserve Ghana's native habitats through programs in national parks, wildlife sanctuaries, and forest reserves. Groups such as Ghana Heritage Conservation Trust (GHCT), Conservation International (CI), Flora & Fauna International (FFI), and the World Wildlife Fund (WWF) are also involved in a number of projects to conserve Ghana's natural wonders.

(Opposite) The Portuguese built Fort Elmina in the 15th century as a base from which to trade for slaves, gold, ivory, and pepper. (Right) This map of the Gold Coast from 1729 shows the settlements of the Ashanti Empire, which ruled the Ghana region until the 1870s.

2 From Empire to Republic

The ancient kingdom of Ghana was located about 500 miles (805 km) north of modern Ghana and included present-day eastern Senegal, southwest Mali, and southern Mauritania. Oral tradition suggests that some of the people who live in present-day Ghana are descendants of the people who lived in these medieval states.

The Akan people, who included the Ashanti (also spelled *Asante*), are believed to have migrated from the ancient kingdom to modern Ghana during the 12th and 13th centuries. There they established several states in the forests of central Ghana. By the beginning of the 1500s, these communities were carrying on a lively trade with the peoples to the north who lived in regions of the southern Sahara. Toward the end of the 16th century, most of the ethnic groups settled in locations where their modern-day descendants still live today.

19

The Gold Coast

Before gaining its independence in 1957, Ghana was called the Gold Coast for its deposits of the precious mineral. In search of gold, ivory, and pepper, Portuguese explorers first arrived on the Gold Coast in 1471. In 1482, they began building the first European structure in the country, a trading fortress they called Elmina ("the Mine"). Soon after, the Gold Coast became the chief supplier of gold to Europe.

By the early 1600s, there was a great demand for slaves to work on European plantations throughout the world. The focus of trade quickly turned from gold to slaves. Over the next several centuries, Dutch, English, Danish, and Swedish traders arrived and the coastline became dotted with European trading fortresses. Conflicts arose between the Europeans as they struggled for control of the slave trade. Sometimes these conflicts involved native peoples as the Europeans sought to ally themselves with various local tribes. In 1642 the Dutch captured Elmina from the Portuguese, who then left the Gold Coast permanently.

While the Europeans competed for control of trade on the Gold Coast, the Ashanti Empire rose to power. The Ashanti people had settled in central Ghana along the crossroads of major trade routes. This allowed them to control trade to the north and south. With the European settlements restricted to the Cape Coast, the Ashanti remained separate and invulnerable, while they also acquired great supplies of arms through trading slaves. By the mid-1700s, the empire was the most powerful state on the Gold Coast. It held this lofty position until Britain began expanding into the central region during the 1870s.

Eventually, the costly power struggle between European groups made trading in slaves less profitable. It took a lot of money and manpower to defend their trading forts from competing traders. Anti-slavery sentiment also increased in Europe during this period. The slave trade subsequently waned, and it was finally banned by Britain in 1808 and Holland in 1814. Eventually, all the European powers except the British were forced out of the Gold Coast.

With the other competition eliminated, the British sought to expand their territory and dominate trade. However, they faced ongoing resistance from the powerful Ashanti. After several battles, the British attacked and burned the Ashanti capital of Kumasi in 1874. Shortly after, they proclaimed the Gold Coast a crown colony. The Ashanti, however, did not submit to colonization and remained an independent nation.

British Rule

The Gold Coast Colony of Great Britain was established on July 24, 1874. It originally consisted of a 62-mile (100-km) strip of land along the coast that extended to the borders of the Ashanti Empire. Three years later the British moved the administrative capital from Cape Coast to Accra, where the people could enjoy a drier climate.

In 1901, the British defeated the Ashanti in their final uprising and the empire was made part of the British colony. Shortly after, the new boundaries of the Gold Coast were established. The Northern Territories (the region north of Ashanti) became a British *protectorate*. Part of German Togoland also became a British territory in 1919 and was joined with the protectorate.

During the first half of the 20th century, the Gold Coast prospered under British rule. Major improvements were seen in the social, economic, and educational fields. The colonial administration created telecommunications and postal services, and the road and railway construction enhanced transportation. New crops were introduced and the economy flourished from the export of cocoa, timber, and gold. By the end of World War I in 1918, the Gold Coast was the most prosperous colony on the African continent.

Growth of Nationalism

As the Gold Coast flourished economically and socially, the power gradually shifted from the British to the Africans. However, this shift was much too slow for most Ghanaians. Formal education and military service had broadened their horizons, and they had come to resent their subservient position. By the 1920s, a strong sense of national unity had developed among ethnic groups of the colony like the Ashanti, the Dagomba, and the Ewe.

The nationalist movement greatly accelerated after World War II (1939–45). At the forefront of civil unrest were the returning veterans who had served Britain with great distinction during the war. They had expected the economy to be flourishing upon their return, but instead encountered widespread shortages of basic necessities, a lack of housing, rising inflation, and widespread unemployment. These economic hardships, combined with ongoing political grievances, fanned the flames of discontent.

During the 1940s, new political parties sprang up all over the Gold Coast. Many shared a common goal—independence. The United Gold Coast Convention (UGCC), founded in 1947, was the first nationalist organization with the goal of self-government "in the shortest possible time." Kwame Nkrumah, an American-educated leader in the *Pan-African* movement, was picked to be the group's general secretary. However, Nkrumah's relationship with the UGCC was a rocky one. He soon grew impatient with the conservative ways of the UGCC and felt that more radical tactics were needed. In 1948 Nkrumah was arrested and jailed along with other UGCC leaders for anti-colonial activities. The party, which did not seek drastic or revolutionary measures to achieve its goals, dismissed Nkrumah from his post. Undaunted, he founded the Convention People's Party (CPP) in June 1949.

Although the UGCC remained active, the CPP more successfully appealed to the working classes and quickly gathered a large following. In contrast to the UGCC's goal of self-government "in the shortest possible time," the CPP called for "self-government *now*." In early 1950, Nkrumah initiated his Positive Action campaign, which included widespread labor strikes and nonviolent protest. However, when violent anti-colonial riots broke out, the CPP was blamed. Once again, Nkrumah and other key members of the CPP were arrested and imprisoned, but this only served to make Nkrumah even more heroic in the eyes of fellow Africans.

The following year, in an effort to curb violent protests, the colonial government created a new constitution. The first elections for the Legislative Assembly under the new constitution were held in February 1951. Although he was still in prison, Nkrumah won the election for the Accra Central seat. The CPP also won two-thirds of the available seats in the Assembly, while the UGCC only won three seats. The party disbanded shortly after the elections.

Later that month, Governor Sir Charles Arden-Clarke released Nkrumah

After a series of violent political uprisings and protests, Ghana was finally granted independence from Great Britain in 1957. Here, the Duchess of Kent reads the English Queen's decree to the Ghanaian National Assembly.

from prison and gave him the title of "leader of government business." This position was similar to that of a prime minister and was an important step toward Ghanaian self-government.

In 1952, the Cabinet replaced the Executive Council and the new position of prime minister was created. Unlike the Executive Council, which fell under the authority of the colonial governor, the Cabinet answered to the Legislative Assembly. In the next election, Nkrumah became the first African prime minister of the colony and was re-elected in the 1954 and 1956 elections. In May 1956, the people of British Togoland (now the Volta and Northern Regions of Ghana) voted to become part of the Gold Coast. One year later, Britain completely relinquished control of the Gold Coast colony.

Independence

On March 6, 1957, Ghana became an independent nation. Just after midnight, a new national flag, bearing the Pan-African colors of red, black, and green, was hoisted in Accra's Black Star Square. Three years later, in 1960, Kwame Nkrumah was named the first president of the new nation. A constitution was written and on July 1, Ghana officially became a republic.

Nkrumah was not a flawless leader, however, and over the next few years he made many mistakes that eventually led to his downfall. First, he started numerous costly projects that further damaged the economy. For example, using future cocoa earnings as security, he took out many loans for machinery and equipment to build factories and refineries. However, global cocoa prices dropped drastically in the following years, destroying the nation's economic stability and forcing Nkrumah to abandon his projects. Second, he suspended the democratic constitution in 1964 and proclaimed himself president for life. He also banned all political parties except for his own and exiled or imprisoned all those who opposed him.

In February 1966, while Nkrumah was on a state visit to China he was overthrown in a nonviolent *coup*. This was the start of a series of coups as

During the 1970s and 1980s, Ghanaian military leader Jerry Rawlings led several coups in a quest for power. He would survive four attempts to overthrow his own government, as well as an attempt on his life.

new civilian governments were overthrown by the military time after time. After Nkrumah's overthrow, a military government called the National Liberation Council (NLC) took power and restored multiparty elections.

In 1969, Edward Akufo-Addo was elected president of Ghana's Second Republic, but the real power lay in the hands of Prime Minister Dr. Kofi Abrefa Busia of the Progress Party (PP). Just three years later, another coup led by the National Redemption Council (NRC) placed the power of government back in military hands for the next seven years. Air Force Flight Lieutenant Jerry John Rawlings led several of these coups. In 1979, he succeeded in overthrowing the military government and oversaw the execution of three former heads of state and dozens of senior military officers. Rawlings stepped down later that year when the people elected Hilla Limann to be president of the Third Republic. However, when economic conditions worsened, Rawlings staged another coup in 1981, this time finding support from Libyan troops.

Following the 1981 coup, Rawlings was named head of state. Like Nkrumah, he suspended the constitution and banned all opposing political parties, an act that gained him many enemies. Rawlings survived four coup attempts as well as an attempted assassination before becoming the first president of the Fourth Republic in 1992. His party, the National Democratic Congress (NDC), won 133 of the 200 seats in Parliament. Four years later, he was re-elected to the presidency.

The constitution would not allow Rawlings to run for president for a third term, and so in 2000 his vice president, John Atta Mills, ran but was defeated by John Agyekum Kufuor of the New Patriotic Party (NPP). President Kufuor officially entered office in January 2001. It was the first peaceful transfer of government in Ghana's tumultuous history.

Since taking his position, Kufuor has set up commissions to address the human rights offenses that occurred during the years of military rule. Jerry Rawlings, who was included among the prosecuted, testified before one of the commissions in February 2004.

John Agyekum Kufuor was elected president of Ghana in 2000. This election marked the first peaceful transfer of power in three decades.

Ghana's 1992 constitution is intended to balance the powers of government among three branches: executive, legislative, and judicial. (Opposite) Ghana's parliament meets in this building in Accra. (Right) The government provides many public services. Here a sign promotes free HIV/AIDS testing outside a government building in Kibi.

3 Governing the Black Star of Africa

After winning its independence, Ghana was hailed as the "black star of Africa," a model of freedom and democracy for the whole continent. However, much of Ghana's history as an independent nation has been marked by political strife. Democracy came and went as various leaders suspended the constitution and banned parties that supported the opposition. As a result, Ghana's turbulent political history has been shaped by four different republics, with each successive republic following a period of military rule.

The Fourth Republic

The fourth and current Republic of Ghana operates under the 1992 constitution, which was put into effect on January 7, 1993. Designed to ensure a balance of power, it was modeled after the governments of Britain and the United States. The new constitution restored multiparty elections and gave people over 18 years of age the right to vote for the country's leaders. The Electoral Commission, also established by the 1992 constitution, is responsible for organizing and overseeing national elections.

Ghana's government consists of three major branches: the executive, legislative, and judiciary. The president heads the executive branch and serves as chief of state, head of government, and commander-in-chief of the armed forces. He or she shares authority with the Council of State and many other advisory organizations, including the National Security Council. Under the constitution, the president is elected to a four-year term and is limited to two terms of office. To win a presidential election, a candidate must win over 50 percent of the votes cast. A run-off election is held if no candidate wins on the first ballot.

The Cabinet consists of the president, vice president, and between 10 and 19 officials who make up the Council of Ministers. These ministers, along with the vice president, are appointed by the president. They advise the president on specific national and international issues, and their ministries are divided into four categories: Governance, Finance and Economy, Infrastructure, and Social Service.

The Council of State consists of 25 citizens who advise the president, Cabinet ministers, members of Parliament, and other government figures on the performance of their duties. For example, when the president appoints a high-ranking public official such as the Commissioner for the Internal Revenue Service or the Inspector General of Police, he seeks the advice of his Council. However, neither the president nor other leaders are obligated to follow the Council's recommendations.

Legislature and Judiciary

The legislative branch of the Ghanaian government consists of a 200-member Parliament, headed by a Speaker. Like the president, members of Parliament are also elected to four-year terms, but there is no limit on the number of terms they can serve. The primary function of Parliament is to make laws and amend bills. Under the constitution, it also has the authority to regulate professional, trade, and business organizations. To pass a law, Parliament must have the approval of the president, who has the power to veto all bills except those with a vote of urgency attached.

The judicial branch operates independently of the other two branches of government and is subject only to the constitution. Its primary functions are to uphold the constitution, enforce the laws of the nation, and administer justice. The *hierarchy* of courts is based largely upon British law and is called the Superior Court of Judicature. It is comprised of the Supreme Court, the Court of Appeal (Appellate Court), the High Court of Justice, and regional tribunals. Parliament may also create lower courts and tribunals as needed.

The Supreme Court is the final court of appeal and makes judgments on constitutional, criminal, and civil cases. It is comprised of a chief justice and no fewer than nine other justices.

Political Parties

After the ban on political parties was lifted in 1992, a number of parties sprang up in Ghana. When the Fourth Republic was first established, eight organizations received their final certificates as official political parties. Some of them are now defunct, while others survived by merging to form new parties. Currently, the two most powerful political groups in Ghana are the New Patriotic Party (NPP) and the National Democratic Congress (NDC).

Most modern-day political parties claim to model their ideals on one of two major parties that emerged after the overthrow of the First Republic: the Convention People's Party (CPP), founded by Kwame Nkrumah, and the Progress Party (PP), founded by Dr. Kofi Busia during the Second Republic. Under Nkrumah, the CPP supported a unified, one-party state. It met with strong opposition from the PP, which supported a democratic state. The New Patriotic Party (NPP), led by President Kufuor, lays claim to the Busia tradition. Its opposition, which includes the Convention People's Party (CPP), the People's National Convention (PNC), and the National Reform Party (NRP), links itself with the Nkrumahist tradition.

Under Ghana's current constitution, ethnically based political parties are prohibited. The goal of most political parties is to uphold the constitution and promote unity among the Ghanaian people, though dissension continues to affect the political and social climate of Ghana.

As part of its anti-corruption efforts, the current NPP government created the National Reconciliation Commission (NRC) in 2002 to investigate human rights violations during Ghana's years of military rule. The NRC is currently engaged in prosecuting several former high-level government officials of the NDC, including former president Jerry John Rawlings. The hearings, part of President Kufuor's policy of zero tolerance for government corruption, have exacerbated the bad feelings between Ghana's rival parties.

Most modern political parties in Ghana take their ideals from earlier Ghanaian movements. This 1957 photo shows a rally of the Convention People's Party (CPP) supporting the implementation of a unified state in Ghana.

Administrative Regions

Ghana is divided into 10 administrative regions, each with its own capital city. These 10 regions are in turn divided into 110 districts, with District Assemblies representing local governments. With the central government, they form the basis of governmental authority in Ghana.

The District Assemblies are divided into three categories, from greatest to smallest population: Metropolitan, Municipal, or District. Currently, there are 3 Metropolitan Assemblies, 4 Municipal Assemblies, and 103 District

Ghana's government provides one of the best systems of public education in Africa. These Ghanaian primary-school students are studying English. Education begins for all children at age six and continues for nine years.

Assemblies. Members of the District Assemblies are elected solely by the residents of each district.

Since implementing the 1992 constitution, Ghana has had a stable democracy and has emerged as a leader in political, social, and economic reform in Africa. However, the fight against poverty remains a primary challenge for the Ghanaian government as the young nation struggles to gain a foothold in the global economy.

(Opposite) A gold worker practices his craft in a streetside shop. Gold is Ghana's number-one export. (Right) Female timber-company workers wear masks to protect their lungs as they work in a sanding shop. The wood they are sanding will be exported for garden furniture.

4 A Hopeful Economy

ALTHOUGH GHANA IS rich with natural resources, it remains one of the poorest countries in Africa. When Ghana achieved its independence, its economy was the strongest in Africa, but it soon began a downward spiral from which the people are still trying to recover. Massive national debts, *unsustainable* agricultural methods, and an unpredictable climate have all contributed to water and food shortages, unemployment, and widespread poverty.

The Economic Recovery Program

In 1983, the administration of Jerry Rawlings launched the Economic Recovery Program (ERP) under the guidance of the International Monetary Fund (IMF). The ERP focused on reducing debt and promoting the export

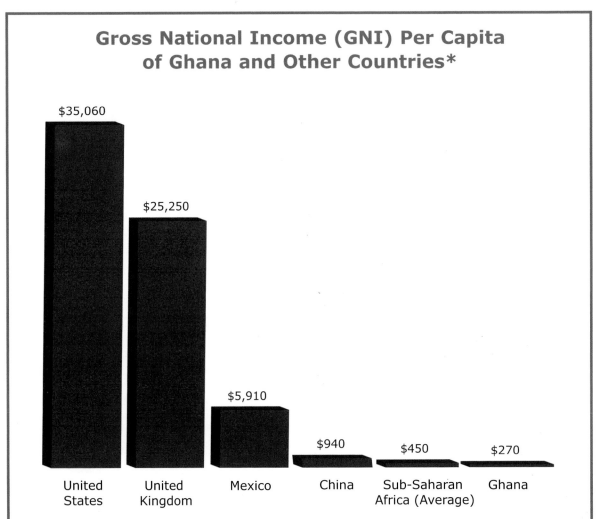

Gross National Income (GNI) Per Capita of Ghana and Other Countries*

- United States — $35,060
- United Kingdom — $25,250
- Mexico — $5,910
- China — $940
- Sub-Saharan Africa (Average) — $450
- Ghana — $270

*Gross national income per capita is the total value of all goods and services produced domestically in a year, supplemented by income received from abroad, divided by midyear population. The above figures take into account fluctuations in currency exchange rates and differences in inflation rates across global economies.

Figures are 2002 estimates. Source: World Bank, 2003.

sector by boosting production. Harsh initiatives of the program included raising taxes and laying off many employees in the civil service. Farmers were paid less money for their crops, and domestic poverty increased. The ERP was very unpopular among most of the people, particularly those who did not work in the export sector.

Eventually, the rigid policies of the ERP reversed the economic decline and sparked a wave of much-needed foreign investments. However, huge debts accumulated since most projects were funded by foreign loans, particularly those from the IMF.

At the end of 2002, Ghana owed $5.8 billion in foreign debts. It ranked 76th in the world in gross domestic product (GDP), the value of all goods and

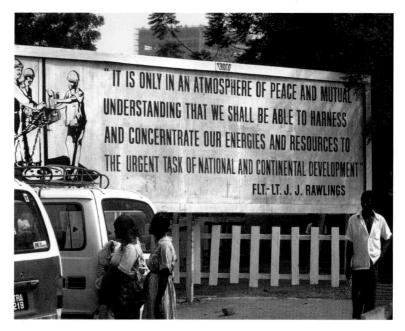

Former Ghanaian president Jerry Rawlings's quote, posted on this billboard, reminds citizens that it will take a national effort to overcome the country's current state of poverty.

services produced by a country in a year. The 2003 *Human Poverty Index*, published by the United Nations Development Programme, ranked Ghana 43rd out of the world's 78 least developed countries.

Agriculture

Agriculture is the backbone of the Ghanaian economy. Of the 9 million people that make up Ghana's workforce, 60 percent are farmers. Most farmers hold small land plots and make their living through subsistence agriculture. They trade with the crops they grow, but generate little or no cash income.

Subsistence farmers grow a variety of dietary staples to feed their families. Traditional crops include yams, plantains, corn, rice, peanuts, millet, sorghum, and *cassava*. Important agricultural exports include cocoa, palm oil, papaya, rubber, spices, bananas, and pineapples. Cocoa is Ghana's most important cash crop and the country's second-largest export earner after gold, accounting for about 13 percent of the GDP. There are about 250,000 cocoa farmers in Ghana; most of them own and operate small farms about five acres in size.

Since the years of colonial rule, cocoa has yielded high returns; by the 1920s the country had been producing more than half of the world's cocoa, and today Ghana remains one of the leading producers of the crop. Ghanaian cocoa is prized for its superb quality. Some major chocolate manufacturers in the United Kingdom and United States use only Ghanaian cocoa in their products.

In a given year, the cocoa sector usually earns between $300 million and $400 million. Cocoa sales reached a record-breaking $889.7 million for the

2002–2003 season, thanks to the second-highest cocoa production total in history at nearly a half-million tons. Since the Ghanaian economy is strongly influenced by export prices and agricultural production levels, this was a major step toward stability.

All of the cocoa grown in Ghana is sold at fixed prices to the Ghana Cocoa Board, called Cocobod. Established in 1947, Cocobod oversees all aspects of the cocoa industry including quality control, marketing and transporting cocoa products, and agricultural research and training.

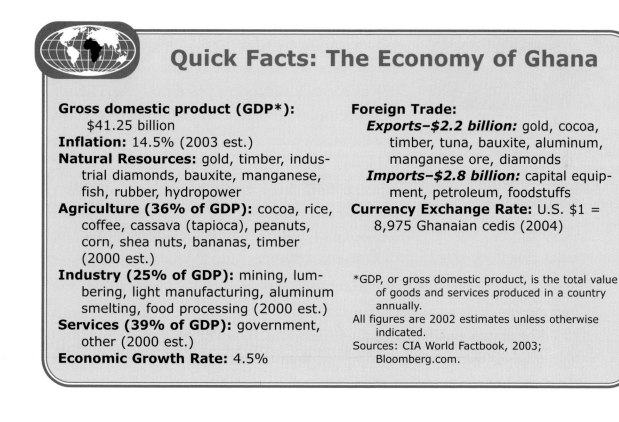

Quick Facts: The Economy of Ghana

Gross domestic product (GDP*):
$41.25 billion

Inflation: 14.5% (2003 est.)

Natural Resources: gold, timber, industrial diamonds, bauxite, manganese, fish, rubber, hydropower

Agriculture (36% of GDP): cocoa, rice, coffee, cassava (tapioca), peanuts, corn, shea nuts, bananas, timber (2000 est.)

Industry (25% of GDP): mining, lumbering, light manufacturing, aluminum smelting, food processing (2000 est.)

Services (39% of GDP): government, other (2000 est.)

Economic Growth Rate: 4.5%

Foreign Trade:
Exports–$2.2 billion: gold, cocoa, timber, tuna, bauxite, aluminum, manganese ore, diamonds

Imports–$2.8 billion: capital equipment, petroleum, foodstuffs

Currency Exchange Rate: U.S. $1 = 8,975 Ghanaian cedis (2004)

*GDP, or gross domestic product, is the total value of goods and services produced in a country annually.

All figures are 2002 estimates unless otherwise indicated.

Sources: CIA World Factbook, 2003; Bloomberg.com.

A woman harvests cocoa pods, which must be picked twice a year when they are ripe. Cocoa is Ghana's second most valuable export.

Industry

The industry sector employs 15 percent of the Ghanaian work force and accounts for 25 percent of the GDP. Much of Ghana's industry centers on processing agricultural products. Major operations include processing cocoa and timber, mining, manufacturing, aluminum smelting, and the production of foods and beverages.

More than 800,000 people work in the cocoa industry. Ghanaian factories process between 18 and 22 percent of the cocoa crop into products such as cocoa butter, cocoa paste, and cocoa liquor for export markets. The remainder is exported in its raw state. Cola nuts, the basic ingredient in many soft drinks, are the source of another vital industry. Cola trees thrive in the same environment as cacao (the tree source of cocoa), and the two are often grown together. Processing the oily nuts of the shea tree into shea butter, which is used in the manufacture of soaps and candles, is an important source of income for farmers from the remote northern areas of the country.

The waters of Ghana teem with life and about 10 percent of the population works in the fishing industry. Traditional fishermen number about 100,000 and some 150,000 more work in so-called downstream industries such as canning factories and trading centers. In 1999, fish and processed seafood products accounted for 20 percent of non-traditional export earnings, bringing in $62 million in foreign exchange. However, overfishing has depleted this important resource to a dangerous level and the tuna export market has recently declined. As a way to boost fish levels, *aquaculture* (raising food fish under controlled conditions) has become a viable industry.

The lush forests of Ghana contribute to another vital industry—timber. The country's third-largest export, timber accounts for 6 percent of the GDP and about 30 percent of export earnings. About 70,000 people work in the timber industry, with some 250,000 more working in related fields such as milling and manufacturing.

Of the 680 tree species that grow in the forests of Ghana, fewer than 10 species account for over 90 percent of Ghana's timber exports. Several traditionally exported prime wood species such as teak, iroko (a high quality hardwood used as a teak substitute), and several types of mahogany are currently in danger of extinction. To conserve this valuable resource, the Ghanaian government sets limits on the number of logs that may be cut in a year.

With one of the largest gold reserves in the world, Ghana has been a global leader in gold exports for centuries. Recently, the precious metal replaced cocoa as the highest export earner, accounting for about 45 percent of export earnings. Most of the gold in Ghana comes from underground mines in the western Ashanti Region. The Obuasi gold mine, which is owned by AngloGold Ashanti, is the richest in the country.

Since Ghana does not have enough money to build its own mining industry, the country must rely heavily on foreign investors. This cuts down

Because the mining and timber industries destroy so much land, Ghana has implemented a reforestation program to help compensate for the destruction. This man is planting trees near a pit that had been mined for manganese.

on the benefits to the local economy. For example, in 2000 gold exports brought in $617 million, or 37 percent of the country's export earnings, but they only contributed 12 percent to the GDP. As set forth by the Minerals and Mining Law of 1986, foreign investors are allowed to keep 25 to 45 percent of their earnings, and they also pay reduced income taxes. Also, with only about 10,000 Ghanaians working in the industry, gold mining doesn't provide many jobs for the local people.

Ghana also has other mineral deposits, though they are not as plentiful as gold. Large diamond reserves are located about 70 miles (113 km) northwest of Accra. Manganese, which is used to make iron and copper alloys, and bauxite, which is the principal ore used to make aluminum, are mined and exported.

Although the mining industry shows good potential for boosting Ghana's economy, many people are concerned about how it can harm the environment. Mining destroys trees, native wildlife habitats, and other natural resources at a frightening rate. It also poisons surface water and groundwater with cyanide and other toxic chemicals. The Ghanaian government is faced with a great challenge as it seeks to achieve a sustainable balance between foreign export earnings and ecological conservation.

Services

The services sector, which accounts for 39 percent of the GDP, is a valuable contributor to the economy. The civil service is Ghana's largest single employer, with about 76,000 civil workers. Many candidates are recruited from Ghana's universities and other educational institutions. All are required to take civil service entrance examinations.

Tourism is the fasting-growing sector of the economy. During the 1990s tourism brought in more foreign earnings than timber. With Ghana's many national parks, wildlife sanctuaries, and forest reserves, *ecotourism* is a fast-growing and promising business. Major tourist attractions include the Mole

National Park in northern Ghana, which covers nearly 200 miles (500 km) and features lions and elephants, and the Kakum National Park in the rain forest of central Ghana.

Hydroelectricity

The Volta River Authority, established in 1961, generates and distributes almost all of Ghana's electricity through two hydroelectric plants on the Volta River. The first hydroelectric plant was completed in 1965 at Akosombo. The second plant at Kpong was completed in 1981.

A series of long-term droughts in 1998 reduced Lake Volta's capacity and caused severe shortages of electrical power throughout the country. In 2000, 70 percent of the Ghanaian people had no electricity. The energy crisis also severely damaged Ghana's industries, particularly aluminum smelting. With support from the World Bank, the Akosombo power station is undergoing an $18-million upgrade that promises to improve conditions. The Volta River Authority is also planning several future hydroelectric projects to keep up with the increasing demand for electrical power.

Although Ghana's economy shows promise, the nation continues to struggle. A crucial and ongoing problem is the lack of safe drinking water. The majority of Ghanaians live in rural areas and about two-thirds of them have no access to safe drinking water. Pressure from the IMF and World Bank recently resulted in the *privatization* of water in order to recover costs. In protest of the water charges, several groups united as the National Coalition Against the Privatization of Water, though they did not change the leaders' minds. With the average Ghanaian earning less than one dollar a day, paying for water is a heavy burden. Global organizations, like WaterAid of Great Britain, work with local groups to build wells and promote water safety and hygiene.

Currently, the Ghanaian government is trying to boost the economy by expanding and diversifying agriculture and industry. Goals include opening more gold refineries and using Ghana's wealth from natural resources to launch more manufacturing ventures. In the agricultural sector, policymakers are encouraging large-scale farming and the export of more nontraditional crops.

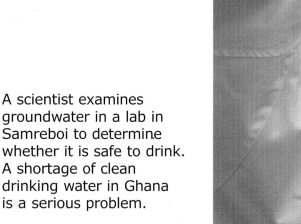

A scientist examines groundwater in a lab in Samreboi to determine whether it is safe to drink. A shortage of clean drinking water in Ghana is a serious problem.

(Opposite) The Ashanti are the largest single tribe in Ghana. These Ashanti women shaved their hair in mourning for a deceased *asantehene*, or tribal king. The *adinkra* cloth they are wearing shows respect and honor to the late king. (Right) Ghanaian girls wearing outfits with the colors of the country's flag dance at a political gathering.

5 A Vibrant Ethnic Tapestry

AKWAABA IS THE traditional Ghanaian word for "welcome," and Ghana boasts a well-deserved reputation for its friendliness and hospitality. The population of over 20 million people is comprised of over 100 ethnic groups, each with its own unique customs. Several African languages are spoken, but since independence English has been the official language. The Ghanaian government chose a neutral language to avoid stirring up conflict between ethnic groups.

Major Ethnic Groups

The Akan are the largest ethnic group in Ghana, comprising about 44 percent of the population. This group includes the Ashanti (the largest single tribe in Ghana), Akuapim, Akyem, Fanti, and Kwahu. All Akan tribes speak

Quick Facts: The People of Ghana

Population: 20,467,747
Ethnic Groups: black African 98.5% (major tribes—Akan 44%, Moshi-Dagomba 16%, Ewe 13%, Ga 8%, Yoruba 1%), European and other 15% (1998)
Age structure:
   0–14 years: 38.9%
   15–64 years: 57.5%
   65 years and over: 3.6%
Population growth rate: 1.45%
Birth rate: 53.02 births/1,000 population
Infant mortality rate: 103.22 deaths/1,000 live births
Death rate: 20.17 deaths/1,000 population

Life expectancy at birth:
   total population: 56.53 years
   male: 55.66 years
   female: 57.43 years
Total fertility rate: 3.32 children born/woman
Religion: indigenous beliefs 21%, Muslim 16%, Christian 63%
Languages: English (official), African languages (including Akan, Moshi-Dagomba, Ewe, and Ga
Literacy: 67.1%

All figures are 2003 estimates unless otherwise indicated.
Source: Adapted from CIA World Factbook, 2003.

Twi (Akan), their traditional language, but each subgroup also has its own regional dialect.

The Akan tribes live mainly in the southern half of the country, in the heart of the Ghanaian rain forest. They were the earliest people to have contact with Europeans and are the most heavily influenced by Western culture and lifestyles. Many joined the churches and attended the schools set up by Protestant missionaries during the 1800s. Today, most Akans are Christians but continue to practice their traditional religions as well. The tribe follows a matrilineal line of descent, which means they trace their genealogy through the mother.

The Dagomba people inhabit the northern regions and speak Dagbani, a language of the Gur family. Subgroups of the Dagomba include the Dagbamba, the Mamprusi, and the Nanumba. Of all the ethnic groups in Ghana, the Dagomba are the least influenced by Western culture and modern lifestyles.

The Dagomba culture shares a rich oral tradition of songs and music, and only recently has the tribe developed a written language. During the 1600s, Arab traders introduced Islam to the region, and today Dagombas are primarily Muslims. Unlike the Akan, the Dagomba is a patrilineal society, tracing the family line through the father.

Other ethnic groups include the Ewe, who live primarily along the eastern border in the Volta Region, and the Ga, who comprise about 8 percent of the population and live mainly in the coastal areas around Accra. Both groups speak a regional dialect of the Kwa language.

Tribal Traditions

Tribal traditions govern all aspects of Ghanaian life. Special rites and rituals mark important turning points such as child naming, puberty initiations, marriage, and death. Many Ghanaians still impart special meaning in the names they choose for their children, marking the days of the week on which they were born. For example, U.N. Secretary-General Kofi Annan, a Ghanaian native, has a Twi name—*kofi* means "born on Friday" and *annan* means "fourth child," signifying that he is the fourth-born child in his family.

In most tribes, land and property are not owned by individuals but are communally owned. Few people become wealthy, but all enjoy the security

A group of Ghanaian mothers with their children. As in many African countries, large extended families often live together in the same home.

of village life, which promotes the even distribution of wealth. Many of Ghana's immigrants are very poor, however, because they have no clan or tribe to rely on during hard times.

In some tribes, only members of certain families can become chiefs. Tribal chiefs are chosen by the people and may be removed if they are not doing a good job. A chief has many responsibilities, including settling disputes, organizing festivals, and ensuring that tribal customs are observed. Among the Dagomba, the symbol of tribal power is a cow skin called the Yendi skin. When a man becomes chief, he is "enskinned," and he is "deskinned" if he is removed. The Ashanti symbol of power is the Golden Stool. An Ashanti man is "enstooled" when he becomes chief and "destooled" if he is removed.

Festivals are an important part of Ghanaian life. Traditional processions, called *durbars*, are the highlight of many festivals. The tribal king or chief dresses in his finest robes and is carried through the city streets in a **palanquin**. Lower chieftains, also decked out in their finest regalia, march or ride behind the king. Musicians, praise singers, and dancers join the procession in a magnificent spectacle of color and sound.

Family Life

Most Ghanaian households are made up of large extended families that typically consist of the mother's relatives. Men are usually the heads of the household, but all family members do their share of work. Women often work as farmers or traders and usually manage the family's money. Those who stay at home raise vegetables for the family to eat and sell any extra produce at the market.

Elders often make traditional craft items such as garments, woodcarvings, or pottery to sell at the market. They are highly respected for their wisdom and perform an important duty by passing on traditional stories to the children. Ghanaian children, particularly girls, perform many household chores such as cooking, cleaning, and gardening. Some children as young as six years old work at after-school jobs to contribute to their family's income.

Although some of the wealthiest Ghanaians live in modern homes with electricity, plumbing, and appliances, most homes have mud walls and a roof that is either thatched or made of iron and asbestos. During the rainy seasons, the walls gradually wear away and homes typically must be rebuilt every five to six years. Many Ghanaian homes are compound houses, which means that the living quarters of several families all surround a central court-yard where the livestock is kept. Houses without courtyards usually have a veranda where many of the daily activities take place.

Ghanaian women take great pride in their cooking skills. Soups are the main dietary staple and are usually made from palm nuts or peanuts (or groundnuts, as Ghanaians call them). Soups are eaten with other traditional dishes, which include *fufu* (pounded plantains, cassava, or yams), *kokonte* (cassava meal cooked into a paste), and *banku* (fermented corn dough). For breakfast, many Ghanaians enjoy *pumpuka*, a type of porridge made of roughly ground millet. Other food staples include rice, fish, and bread.

Education

Ghana boasts one of the finest educational systems in West Africa. It is similar to the U.S. school system. Tuition is free for the first nine years, and everyone must attend school until at least the ninth grade.

Children start attending school at age six. After completing six years of elementary school, students move on to three years of junior high school. There the academic program is combined with vocational and technical training, which either prepares students for entry into the job market or for the next three years of senior secondary school (the equivalent to a U.S. high school). Senior secondary schools have tuition fees, and though Ghanaians place great value on education, about one-quarter of the students drop out because they can't afford it. Those students who can attend and graduate must take an entrance examination before entering one of Ghana's universities.

Soccer

Soccer is the national sport and Ghana's teams are tough competitors. The best players in the country join the Black Stars, Ghana's national soccer team. They have one of the best records of any African team, having won the African Nations Cup four times between 1963 and 1982. However, the team has not yet qualified for the World Cup, the most prestigious international tournament.

Playing soccer was once taboo for Ghanaian females because people believed it made them incapable of having children. However, now the women have their own national team called the Black Queens. The team began rising in the international women's soccer ranks in the early 1990s. By 1998, they had placed second in the African Women's Championship of that year. They placed third in the 2000 championship, and second again in 2002.

Today, children all over Ghana enjoy playing soccer, yet soccer balls are also hard to come by and many children can't afford shoes. A variety of charitable organizations, such as the PLAY SOCCER program, are working to provide equipment and promote the popular sport.

A member of Ghana's Black Star soccer team watches a game from the sidelines during a tournament. Soccer is the national sport of Ghana.

Arts

Ghanaians express themselves and celebrate important occasions through music, dance, and drama. Ghanaian music can be divided into three categories: traditional music, which is played during festivals, funerals, and other tribal events; highlife music, which is a blend of traditional and modern styles of other countries; and choral music, which includes hymns and gospels and is usually played in concert halls, schools, and churches. Traditional instruments include gongs, rattles, xylophones, and an assortment of drums.

Accra-born musician King Bruce (1922–98) was a famous composer of classic highlife music. Heavily influenced by American jazz and swing, Bruce released a number of highlife hits between the 1950s and 1990s. In addition to being a senior civil servant and celebrated bandleader, Bruce also helped organize all three of Ghana's musician's unions, including the present-day Musicians Union of Ghana (MUSIGA), formed in 1974.

In addition to a well-rounded heritage of music, dance, and drama, Ghanaians also share a fine tradition of fine arts. One of Ghana's most celebrated artists is Kofi Antubam (1922–64). During the 1960s, the Nkrumah government commissioned Antubam to create a variety of projects that represented Ghana's new national identity. Taking his inspiration from traditional Akan symbols, Antubam designed and created important national artifacts such as the doors to Ghana's Parliament House chambers, the Ghana Mace (a symbol of parliamentary authority), and the Seat of State, a stool used by the Ghanaian president that was modeled after the Golden Stool of the Ashanti kings.

Antubam recruited Ghana's finest artists to help with these projects.

Among them was renowned wood-carver Kojo Bambir from Ghana's Central Region. During the 1950s, the Ghana National Museum in Accra commissioned Bambir to carve important artifacts such as the Akan *abusua poma* (clan or family staff). Many of his works have served as gifts from the Ghanaian government to visiting foreign dignitaries.

The Ghanaian people are known for their skill in an array of traditional crafts including wood-carving, weaving, pottery, and **metallurgy**. The most famous of all Ghanaian crafts is *kente*, the national cloth of Ghana. The name *kente* derives from the Akan *kenten*, meaning "basket." Hand-woven from narrow strips of cotton or silk, the cloth is made with many colors and patterns. Each tribe or clan has its own pattern, which also reveals the rank of the person wearing it. For funerals, most people wear dark kente cloth, but for festive occasions like weddings and birthdays they prefer bright colors. Made by both the Ashanti and Ewe peoples, the special cloth was once worn only by kings; today, it is worn all over the world. Vibrant and unique, kente cloth is much like the diverse yet interwoven ethnic groups of Ghana.

Kente cloth is handwoven for special occasions, like weddings. This bride is wearing a purple kente outfit for her special day.

(Opposite) Buyers and sellers carrying their wares make their way down to the Kumasi market by following the train tracks. Kumasi is Ghana's second-largest city. (Right) The streets of Accra bustle with people. Once a collection of small trading villages, Accra is now a major center of international commerce and the capital of Ghana.

6 Ghana's Cities: Tradition and Innovation

MORE GHANAIANS LIVE in rural areas than in urban areas, but the country's cities are growing quickly. In 2003, the United Nations' Population Division reported that over 45 percent of the population lived in urban areas, which usually have electricity, plumbing, and sewage. These facilities, in combination with Ghana's growing industrial and manufacturing sectors, lure more people to the cities each year.

Accra

The capital city of Accra is also Ghana's largest city. Located in the Eastern Region, it is the administrative, communications, and economic hub of the country. The population in Accra escalated in just 20 years from 867,500 in 1984 to 1.72 million residents in 2004. Major industries in Accra include processing agricultural products, refining petroleum, assembling vehicles and appliances, and manufacturing.

The earliest inhabitants of Accra were the Ga, who built several small villages along the coast. During the 17th century, Accra grew into a thriving town serving the Dutch, Danish, and British trading forts in the region. Major European settlements of the period include Ussher Town (Dutch), Christiansborg Castle (Danish), and James Town (English). Many of these settlements still stand as tourist attractions, and Christiansborg Castle (also called Osu Castle) has even become the seat of the state government. When the British moved their administrative capital to Accra in 1877, the city began expanding to accommodate the newly arrived European residents.

Located on the coast and linked by roads, railways, and an airport to other major cities, Accra is the transportation hub of Ghana. During the 1920s the colonial governor, Sir Frederick Gordon Guggisberg, created a 10-year development program for the country that resulted in major improvements in transportation and other fields. The first important railroad was completed in 1923 and linked Accra, the major shipping port of the period, with Kumasi, the country's cocoa-producing region. Today, Accra's Kotoka International Airport serves the international travel needs of the country. It is one of only five African airports that send planes directly to the United States.

A sprawling city with buildings as diverse as its residents, Accra has architecture is a delightful blend of modern, colonial, and traditional African styles. Christiansborg Castle is the city's most famous historical structure. Other notable sites include the Accra Central Library, the Ghana National Museum, and the Museum of Science and Technology, all of which were built in the middle of the 20th century. Black Star Square, in downtown Accra, is the site of the Eternal Flame of African Liberation. Lit by Kwame Nkrumah on Ghana's first Independence Day, this candle still burns today. On the outskirts of Accra is Achimota School, the country's leading secondary school. The University of Ghana, founded in 1948, is located just north of the city in Legon.

Ghana's very first cocoa farm, planted by Tetteh Quarshie, is also located north of Accra. In 1879, Quarshie brought a single cocoa pod home from Fernando Po, a Spanish island in the Gulf of Guinea, to start his farm. His trees flourished and other Ghanaian farmers bought cocoa pods from him to start their own farms. Cocoa cultivation quickly spread to other parts of the Eastern Region, and from these humble beginnings, Ghana's thriving cocoa industry emerged.

Kumasi

Kumasi is the capital of the Ashanti Region. With a population of about 630,000 in 2004, it is Ghana's second-largest city. Often called "the Garden City" because of its abundance of tropical trees and plants, Kumasi is one of the most beautiful cities in Ghana.

Located in a dense forest belt in the heart of the country's cocoa-producing region, Kumasi is the commercial and transportation link between Accra and the northern regions. It is one of the most prosperous cities in Ghana and produces the majority of the country's primary exports. The main industries of the city are food processing (particularly cocoa products), timber, and mining.

The earth beneath the Ashanti Region is rich with minerals, and gold-

The Ashanti king's Golden Stool is kept locked up most of the time, and is only brought out for special occasions. The Ashanti Region is located in south-central Ghana.

smithing is a popular local craft. The villages surrounding Kumasi also offer a rich array of traditional crafts. Bonwire is famed for its kente cloth, Pankrono for its pottery, and Ahwiaa for wood-carving. Ntonso is renowned for *adinkra* cloth, which is traditionally printed by stamping the cloth with carved wooden blocks.

The city was founded during the 1700s by the *asantehene* (king) of the Ashanti, Osei Tutu. According to Ashanti oral history, Osei Tutu determined the location as the kingdom's capital by planting three *kum* seeds in different areas of the forest. Only one seed sprouted and flourished, eventually growing into a shady tree under which the king and his people often sat. The king thus named the new Ashanti capital Kumasi, a word meaning "where the *kum* tree survived."

Kumasi is the cultural heart of Ghana and boasts many attractions. The National Cultural Center is a huge complex that includes an Ashanti cultural museum, a library dedicated to Ashanti culture and arts, and an exhibition hall where traditional performances are held. Visitors can also see the Asantehene's Palace. The Golden Stool of the Ashanti Kingdom is kept hidden away in the palace and is only brought out on special occasions. The current Ashanti king,

Otumfuo Osei Tutu II, lives in a more modern palace behind the original one. Visitors who bring him a gift and politely ask for an audience are sometimes allowed to meet him.

Sekondi-Takoradi

The capital of the Western Region, Sekondi-Takoradi, is located in southwestern Ghana on the coast. It was formed when the colonial government *amalgamated* the cities of Takoradi and Sekondi in 1946. This twin city was the country's first deepwater seaport.

Both cities developed around European forts built in the 17th century. Sekondi, the older of the two cities, expanded rapidly after the construction of the Accra-Kumasi railway helped it become a primary trade center. Takoradi was an undeveloped fishing village until the seaport was constructed during the 1920s. Today, Sekondi-Takoradi is the industrial and transportation hub of the Western Region. Chief industries include shipbuilding and railroad repair, lumber and cocoa processing, cigarette manufacturing, and fishing.

Tamale

The country's third-largest city, Tamale, is the capital of the Northern Region. An estimated 290,000 people were reported to live in the city in 2004. Located in the savanna region, Tamale has limited natural resources, but it serves as the major industrial, transportation, and administrative hub of northern Ghana. Farming (particularly cotton and cereal grains) and cattle raising are the major occupations of the surrounding region. Most of the city's residents work in agricultural industries, such as the processing of shea nuts and cotton.

The British founded Tamale during the early 1900s as their major administrative center for the colony's northern territories. Today, Tamale is the educational as well as the commercial nucleus of northern Ghana. In the northwestern part of the city lies Education Ridge, where over 20 schools are located. The University of Developmental Studies, northern Ghana's only university, has a curriculum that focuses on agriculture and science.

Tema and Cape Coast

With a population of about 263,000 people in 2004, Tema is Ghana's fourth-largest city. Located on the southeastern coast near Accra, it was originally a small fishing village. An artificial harbor was completed in 1960 and a shipping port was opened the following year. Soon after, Tema developed into the country's busiest shipping port with a vital role in the Ghanaian economy, earning the nickname "gateway to West Africa."

The harbor docks are filled with activity as cocoa and other exports are loaded onto ships waiting to be transported to markets around the world. All around the city are factories and warehouses that busily process items for export. Major industries of the city include processing cocoa and bauxite, aluminum and bauxite smelting, and oil refining. Tema's manufacturing industries include chemicals, textiles, food products, and plastics.

Though Cape Coast is not one of Ghana's largest cities, it is one of the most historic. Located on the Gulf of Guinea, it was the original colonial capital. Now Cape Coast is the capital of Ghana's Central Region and is famed for its beautiful beaches, which are dotted with historical forts and castles.

A Ewe chief overlooks his court. The Ewe live primarily along the eastern border in the Volta Region.

Located near the city are Elmina fortress, the first European structure built south of the Sahara, and Cape Coast Castle, which served as Britain's main slave trading post. Although the castle is a popular tourist attraction, many visitors are haunted by what they see. The dank dungeon walls still bear the scratches of thousands of slaves who were imprisoned there.

Each of Ghana's cities offers unique opportunities to learn about the country's heritage and complex history. Much like Ghanaians, these cities marry cultural tradition with modern innovation.

A Calendar of Ghanaian Festivals

Festivals are a vital and exciting part of Ghanaian life. Rooted in ancient religious traditions, some festivals are linked to natural events such as hunting and harvesting. Others are held to honor ancestors or celebrate historic events. Most Ghanaian festivals are held in the same month every year, but the days are subject to change depending on the chiefs' arrangements or time of harvest.

The Adae Festival is one of the most important ceremonies of the Akan people. It is held throughout the year on every sixth Sunday to honor the spirits of departed ancestors and tribal kings. A colorful *durbar,* or reception, of chiefs wraps up the festivities.

January

New Year's Day, on January 1, is a state holiday and marks the last day of **Kwanzaa**. It is a time of quiet personal reflection and recommitment to cultural values. Gifts are usually given to children and must include a book (preferably on a cultural topic) and a heritage symbol. Public celebrations include a spectacular durbar of tribal chiefs and queen mothers.

The **Edina Bronya Festival** is a native version of Christmas celebrated by the people of Elmina (also known as Edina) on the first Thursday of the New Year. Influenced by the Portuguese settlers who held a similar celebration in January, it's a time to purify oneself and honor ancestors.

Every January people from all over Ghana don their finest costumes and travel to Winneba in the Central Region to celebrate the colorful **Masqueraders Festival**. During the third week in January, the people of Akpafu in the Volta Region celebrate the rice harvest with the **Rice Festival**.

February

The Ashanti people celebrate the **Papa Festival** in the city of Kumawu each year. The event features a grand durbar of chiefs and is intended to inspire courage in children.

On February 24, Ghanaians celebrate **Liberation Day**, commemorating the overthrow of the Nkrumah government in 1966.

March

March 6 is Ghana's **Independence Day**, a national holiday observing the country's liberation from colonial rule in 1957. A festive celebration is held each year in Black Star Square. Highlights include performances, military parades, and a huge durbar of chiefs from all over the country.

May

Celebrated by Ghana's northern tribes, the **Bugum Festival** (Fire Carnival) is linked to Islamic traditions. The highlight of the event is a torch-lit procession that illuminates the streets with dazzling sparks of light. Music and dancing take place until the wee hours of the morning.

May's public holidays include **May Day**, observed on May 1 and honoring the country's laborers, and **Africa Unity Day**, celebrated on May 24.

66

A Calendar of Ghanaian Festivals

June

On June 10, African Americans living in Ghana gather to share their heritage at the **Apiba Festival**. The celebration takes places at Senya Beraku in the Central Region.

July

July 1 is **Republic Day**, a national holiday commemorating the day Ghana officially became a republic in 1960. Festive beach parties are held all over the coast.

The first Tuesday in July brings the fabulous **Bakatue Festival**, a celebration to welcome in the fishing season. Held each year in the coastal city of Elmina, the festival includes a time to make offerings to the gods, a spectacular durbar of chiefs, and a canoe race.

The **Panafest** is a weeklong cultural festival of African music, dance, and performing arts, held every two years to commemorate the experiences of the African people and promote ethnic unity. One of the major events during the week is the **Emancipation Day** ceremony, which marks the end of slavery. It includes a candlelight vigil at the Cape Coast Castle and a majestic durbar of chiefs.

August

Through the entire month of August the Ga people of the Greater Accra Region celebrate the **Homowo Festival**. *Homowo* means "hooting at hunger," and the festival remembers a period of a great famine that ended with an abundant supply of fish and grain. Highlights of the celebration include a procession through Accra. People also have *kpokpoi*, a special dish made with ground corn.

September

Odwira is a celebration of thanksgiving for the yam harvest. Held each year in Akuapim in the Eastern Region, it's a time of ancestral remembrance and renewal of family and social ties.

November

The Ashanti people celebrate the final Adae Festival of the year with **Adae Kese**, meaning "big Adae." Highlights of the event include a display of sacred traditional objects and the firing of muskets.

December

The Builsa people of the Upper East Region celebrate the **Fiok (War) Festival** to commemorate their exploits in battle. There are reenactments of famous battles, and amid war drums and dances, the people pray for protection and a bountiful harvest.

Regardless of their religious beliefs, most Ghanaians celebrate **Christmas** on December 25. Houses are brightly decorated and Christmas trees (often mango, guava, or cashew) are decorated in courtyards. Traditional Christmas Eve dinners feature specially cooked rice eaten with goat or chicken stew or traditional soups. Children often receive gifts like imported treats, books, or new clothes.

67

Recipes

Hkatenkwan (Peanut Stew)

1 whole chicken, cut into pieces
1-inch chunk of fresh ginger, peeled (or 1 tsp. ground ginger)
1 large onion, cut in half (leave one half uncut and chop the other)
1 Tbsp. peanut, palm, or other light vegetable oil
1 Tbsp. tomato paste
1 large tomato, chopped
2/3 cups smooth peanut butter
1 tsp. powdered red pepper or cayenne
1 medium eggplant, peeled and cubed
1 cup fresh or frozen okra, sliced
1 tsp. salt

Directions:
1. Place chicken pieces, ginger, and onion half in large deep skillet. Cover with cold water and bring to a boil. Skim often and turn heat to medium when water boils.
2. While chicken cooks, place oil in a large pot on low heat. Add tomato paste and fry for about five minutes. Add chopped onions and tomatoes and cook, stirring occasionally until onions are clear and soft.
3. Turn off heat under chicken skillet. Carefully remove partially cooked pieces and add to vegetable pot along with half of the chicken stock. (Discard ginger and onion half.)
4. Add peanut butter, salt, and pepper. Cook, stirring occasionally, for about five minutes until peanut butter dissolves.
5. Add eggplant and okra. Simmer uncovered until chicken is cooked and vegetables are tender. Add more broth as needed to maintain a thick stew-like consistency.

Ghanaians usually eat this dish with fufu.

Abenkwan (Palm Oil Soup)

1 cup red palm oil (no substitutes; available at African, international, or health food stores and some supermarkets)
1 medium onion, chopped
1/2 tsp. powdered red pepper or cayenne
1 large tomato, chopped
1 cup fresh or frozen okra, sliced
1 medium eggplant, peeled and cubed
1/2 tsp. salt
1 lb. fish, shellfish, or crabmeat

Directions:
1. Boil the palm oil on high heat in a large heavy cooking pot for five minutes. Add onions and red pepper and cook for another five minutes.
2. Reduce heat to medium-low and add tomato and okra. Simmer uncovered, stirring occasionally, for about an hour until vegetables are soft and soup thickens.
3. Add salt and seafood, and simmer for 15–20 minutes until seafood is cooked. (Cooking time will depend on type of seafood used; don't overcook!)
4. Serve hot over steamed rice. (If soup surface is too oily, skim before serving.)

Hkatenkwan and *abenkwan* recipes adapted from *African News Cookbook: African Cooking for Western Kitchens,* edited by Tami Hultman. New York: Penguin, 1986.

Yam Fufu

1 lb. yams
1 tsp. salt
1/2 tsp. black pepper
1 tsp. butter or margarine

Directions:

1. Wash yams, place in a large pot, and cover with cold, unsalted water. Bring to a boil and cook on medium-high heat for 25–30 minutes or until yams are soft.
2. Drain hot water from pot and fill with cold water to cool yams. When cool enough to handle, peel and cube yams.
3. Place cubed yams back into pot and add pepper and butter. Mash yams with a potato masher or a large wooden spoon until smooth. Mash and stir with all your might; fufu should have a sticky, dough-like consistency.
4. With clean wet hands, form fufu into balls about 2 inches in size.

Fufu can be eaten as is (served warm) or added to cooked soups or stews.

Coconut Ice Cream Balls with Strawberry-Pineapple Sauce

1 qrt. vanilla ice cream
1 cup shredded coconut
1/2 cup strawberry jam
1/2 cup pineapple ice cream topping
1/4 cup sweet wine or brandy (optional)

Directions:

1. Use an ice cream scoop and clean dry hands to make ice cream balls. (You can make as many as you like; the sauce recipe is enough for about 8 balls.) Quickly place each ball on a chilled cookie sheet or tray in the freezer as you make it.
2. Put coconut into a medium bowl. Remove ice cream balls, and one at a time, quickly roll each in coconut until completely coated and return to freezer.
3. In a small bowl, mix jam, ice cream topping, and wine or brandy (if using).
4. Just before serving, evenly divide sauce into serving dishes. Put ice cream balls on top of sauce and serve chilled.

Adapted from Bea Sandler, *The African Cookbook.* New York: Carol Publishing Group, 1993.

Glossary

amalgamate—to combine or unite.

aquaculture—the science of cultivating food fish or shellfish under controlled conditions.

biodiversity hotspot—an area that features exceptional concentrations of diverse species.

breeding birds—birds that breed in a particular country, but do not winter there.

cassava—a starch made by leaching and drying the root of the cassava plant; the source of tapioca, a staple food in tropical regions.

copra—the dried white flesh of the coconut from which coconut oil is extracted.

coup—a sudden overthrow of government, illegally or by force.

deciduous—trees that shed their leaves during certain seasons (usually autumn).

dissected plateau—a former plateau into which numerous valleys were carved by erosion.

ecotourism—a form of tourism in which people travel to areas of ecological interest to observe and learn about native habitats and wildlife.

hierarchy—a chain of command in which leaders are ranked according to ability or status.

Human Poverty Index—compiled by the United Nations, a measure of three areas of human development: longevity (length of life), life expectancy, and a decent standard of living.

metallurgy—the art of extracting, smelting, refining, and creating useful or artistic objects from metals.

palanquin—an enclosed seat or couch that is carried on the shoulders of people and usually transports an important figure like a chief or king.

Pan-African—relating to the nations of Africa; advocating freedom and independence for African people.

privatization—the practice of transferring government or public ownership of an enterprise to private ownership.

protectorate—a relationship in which a superior power protects a dependent country or region from invasion and shares governmental authority.

savanna—flat grassland in a tropical or subtropical region.

tsetse flies—blood-sucking African flies that transmit deadly diseases, including sleeping sickness, to livestock and humans.

unsustainable—relating to an agricultural practice that will not continually provide ongoing products without damaging the environment.

Project and Report Ideas

Report Ideas

Find pictures of one example for each of the following endangered species found in Ghana: mammal, bird, butterfly, and tree. Write three or four paragraphs about each and paste the appropriate picture beside your text.

Find pictures of the following Ghanaian presidents: Kwame Nkrumah, Edward Akufo-Addo, Hilla Limann, Jerry John Rawlings, and John Agyekum Kufuor. Write a two- or three-paragraph biography on each and paste the coinciding picture next to your text.

Presentations

Find a label of a food product made from one of Ghana's major agricultural exports. Paste the label to the top of your page, and underneath it, write four or five paragraphs about the export (where it is grown, how it is processed, etc.) and present it to your class.

Find examples of the three main types of Ghanaian music: traditional, highlife, and choral. Play selections of each for the class and give an oral report on the history of the music and its most popular musicians. Be sure to cover how the styles differ from one another, and your personal opinion of each.

Geography Map

Draw a large map of Ghana on poster board or white cardboard. Color each of the five major geographical regions in a different color. Include a color key beside the map to identify each region. Use dot stickers to indicate the capitals of the 10 administrative regions. Paste small labels by each dot and write the name of the capital and the population for each.

Project and Report Ideas

Creative Projects

Weave a sample of kente cloth on the top half of a piece of white construction paper. Cut straight horizontal lines across the paper, 1/2-inch apart, leaving a 1-inch border on the top and sides. Cut colorful strips of construction paper, weave the strips through the slots in a pleasing pattern, and glue the ends to hold it in place. Below your sample, write four or five paragraphs about kente cloth.

Find as many pictures as you can of Ghana's major economic products and paste them on poster board. Include both natural (e.g., plants) and refined products (e.g., food/beverages).

Draw and color the Ghanaian flag on the top half of a piece of white construction paper. On the bottom half of the page, write three or four paragraphs about the history of Ghana's struggle for independence and what the colors of the flag symbolize.

Chronology

A.D. 1100s–1200s	According to oral tradition, the people of the ancient kingdom of Ghana migrate south to present-day Ghana.
Late 1400s	The first Europeans arrive in Ghana; the Portuguese build the Elmina trading fortress.
1500s–1600s	The slave trade expands; Dutch, British, Danish, and Swedish traders arrive to take part; violent conflicts take place between the European groups.
1600s–1700s	The Ashanti Empire unifies and rises to power.
1800s	The slave trade ends and all Europeans except the British depart Ghana.
1873–74	The British crush numerous Ashanti uprisings and finally capture Kumasi.
1874	The British formally establish the boundaries of the Gold Coast colony.
1901	The Ashanti Empire is officially declared part of the Gold Coast colony.
1900–1940	The Gold Coast prospers under British rule.
1902	Northern Territories are proclaimed a British protectorate.
1919	Part of German Togoland joins the Gold Coast.
1947	The United Gold Coast Convention is founded.
1952	Kwame Nkrumah is elected first African prime minister of the Gold Coast colony.
1956	British Togoland (now the Volta and Northern Regions of Ghana) becomes part of Gold Coast; British Parliament approves CPP's motion for independence.
1957	Gold Coast Colony becomes independent nation of Ghana on March 6.
1960	Ghana becomes a republic on July 1; Kwame Nkrumah becomes the first president.
1964	Nkrumah suspends constitution, declares Ghana a one-party state, and proclaims himself president for life.

1966	Nkrumah is overthrown in nonviolent coup led by Ghanaian military and police forces; the National Liberation Council assumes the new military government.
1969	The Progress Party wins National Assembly elections; Kofi Abrefa Busia is elected prime minister of the Second Republic; Akufo-Addo is elected president.
1972	The National Redemption Council takes power.
1979	Flight Lieutenant Jerry John Rawlings leads a violent military coup of government; Hilla Limann and his People's National Party win elections.
1981	Rawlings stages his second coup and establishes himself chairman of Provisional National Defence Council.
1983	The Rawlings administration launches the Economic Recovery Program.
1992	In response to calls for a civilian government, a new constitution is approved; registration of official political parties begins; Rawlings is elected president.
1996	Rawlings is re-elected president.
1998	Former U.S. president Bill Clinton visits Ghana during his tour of Africa; drought causes low water levels, resulting in a national energy crisis.
2000	John Kufuor of the New Patriotic Party is elected Ghana's new president.
2001	Ghana accepts an IMF/World Bank plan for debt relief.
2003	Cocoa sector earns record-breaking $889.7 million during 2002/2003 season and enjoys second-highest production rate in history.
2004	The World Bank announces it will support Ghana with one billion dollars for social and economic improvements under a four-year program.
2009	To help small farmers threatened by the global economic slowdown, the government accepts $27 million in aid from the Alliance for Green Revolution in Africa.

Further Reading/Internet Resources

Ahiagble, Gilbert Bobbo, and Louise Meyer. *Master Weaver from Ghana*. Seattle, Wash.: Open Hand Publishing, 1998.

Briggs, Philip. Ghana, 2nd: *The Bradt Travel Guide*. Chalfont St. Peter, England: Bradt Travel Guides, 2001.

Gaines, James. *12 Days in Ghana: Reunions, Revelations and Reflections*. Bloomington, Ind.: 1stBooks Library, 2002.

Naylor, Rachel. *Ghana (Oxfam Country Profiles)*. Oxford, England: Oxfam Academic, 2000.

Oppong, Joseph R., and Esther D. Oppong. *Ghana (Modern World Nations)*. Philadelphia: Chelsea House Publishers, 2003.

Travel Information

http://travel.state.gov/travel/cis_pa_tw/cis/cis_1124.html
http://www.lonelyplanet.com/destinations/africa/ghana/
http://www.ghanaembassy.nl/

History and Geography

https://www.cia.gov/library/publications/the-world-factbook/geos/gh.html
http://lcweb2.loc.gov/frd/cs/ghtoc.html#gh0004
http://www.ghanaweb.com/GhanaHomePage/history/
http://cyberschoolbus.un.org/infonation/index.asp

Culture and Festivals

http://www.africaguide.com/country/ghana/culture.htm#music
http://pbskids.org/africa/myworld/westafrica.html

Publisher's Note: The websites listed on this page were active at the time of publication. The publisher is not responsible for websites that have changed their address or discontinued operation since the date of publication. The publisher reviews and updates the websites each time the book is reprinted.

President of Ghana
P.O. Box 1627
Osu, Accra
Ghana
E-mail: castle@idngh.com

Ghana Speaker of the Parliament
Ghana Parliament House
Accra, Ghana
Tel.: (+233) 21668514
E-mail: parclerk@ghana.com

Ghana Tourist Board
Executive Director
Ghana Tourist Board
P.O. Box 3106
Accra, Ghana
Tel.: (+233) 21222153
Fax: (+233) 21231779

Embassy of Ghana
3512 International Drive, NW
Washington, DC 20008
Tel.: (202) 686-4520
Fax: (202) 686-4527
Web site: http://www.ghana-embassy.org/

Ghana National Chamber of Commerce
65, Kojo Thompson Road, First Floor
Standard Chartered Bank Building
Tudu Branch, P.O. Box 2325
Accra, Ghana
Tel.: (+233) 21662427
Fax: (+233) 21662210

Index

Numbers in **bold italic** refer to captions.

Index

Contributors/Picture Credits

Professor Robert I. Rotberg is Director of the Program on Intrastate Conflict and Conflict Resolution at the Kennedy School, Harvard University, and President of the World Peace Foundation. He is the author of a number of books and articles on Africa, including *A Political History of Tropical Africa* and *Ending Autocracy, Enabling Democracy: The Tribulations of Southern Africa*.

Barbara Aoki Poisson is the author of *The Ainu of Japan*, a nonfiction children's book about Japan's first peoples. She is a freelance journalist who's published hundreds of articles in newspapers and magazines such as *The Mariner*, *The Antiquer*, and *Family Fun*. She was born in Fukuoka City, Japan, and lives in Leonardtown, Maryland.

Page
2:    © OTTN Publishing
7:    © OTTN Publishing
8:    Markus Matzel/Das Fotoarchiv
10:   Marion Kaplan Photography
11:   Gallo Images/Corbis
16:   Ron Giling/Das Fotoarchiv
18:   Friedrich Stark/Das Fotoarchiv
19:   Das Fotoarchiv
24:   Central Press/Getty Images
26:   Hulton/Archive/Getty Images
27:   Michel Porro/Getty Images
28:   Marion Kaplan Photography
29:   Markus Matzel/Das Fotoarchiv
33:   Mark Kauffman/Time Life Pictures/Getty Images
34:   Sean Sprague/Das Fotoarchiv
36:   Marion Kaplan Photography
37:   Ron Giling/Das Fotoarchiv
38:   © OTTN Publishing
39:   William F. Campbell/Time Life Pictures/Getty Images
42:   Lineair Fotoarchief/Das Fotoarchiv
44:   Ron Giling/Das Fotoarchiv
47:   Ron Giling/Das Fotoarchiv
48:   Marion Kaplan Photography
49:   Marion Kaplan Photography
52:   Lineair Fotoarchief/Das Fotoarchiv
55:   Wolfgang Schmidt/Das Fotoarchiv
57:   Sean Sprague/Das Fotoarchiv
58:   Marion Kaplan Photography
59:   William F. Campbell/Time Life Pictures/Getty Images
62:   Henning Christoph/Das Fotoarchiv
65:   Henning Christoph/Das Fotoarchiv

Cover photos: Corel (5 photos); Cartesia Software; Corbis
Cover design by Dianne Hodack, Harding House Publishing Service, Inc.